Dancing
with the
Scars

Dancing with the Scars

From Failures to Faith

Twanna Henderson

Dancing with the Scars
by Twanna Henderson

Cover Design by Atinad Designs.

© Copyright 2013

SAINT PAUL PRESS, DALLAS, TEXAS

First Printing, 2013

The name SAINT PAUL PRESS and its logo are registered as a trademark in the U.S. patent office.

ISBN-10: 0-9849441-3-3
ISBN-13: 978-0-9849441-3-2

Printed in the U.S.A.

ACKNOWLEDGMENTS

To the man who has always encouraged me to walk in my giftedness: My husband, Rev. Dr. Michael L. Henderson, Sr. Thank you for your love, your support, your leadership, your covering, and your affirmation. You're a blessing to my life.

To my parents who left this earth much too early: Willie and Geraldine Taylor. Thank you for instilling in me that I can do all things through God.

To my siblings for their continual support of me: Minister Willette Robinson, Edward Taylor, and Camille Taylor. Thanks for being in my corner.

To my spiritual mother: Rev. Dr. Jo Ann Browning. Thank you for being a true woman of God who is unselfish in her mentoring.

To those sisters in Christ who I have mentored and shared with over the years: Thank you for allowing me to share aspects of my testimony with you. I pray that it has helped you along the way.

To my prayer warriors: You know who you are. Thank you for praying this book into existence.

To everyone who has helped to extend my reach: Thank you.

To my son, MJ: Thank you for being the wind beneath my wings. This would not have come into fruition without you.

CONTENTS

PROLOGUE

Born to Dance

I remember writing my first book when I was around seven or eight years old. I carefully and meticulously stapled the edges together, folded two sheets of white paper and gently stapled the center. I grabbed a fat #2 pencil and began writing my life story. After writing about the details of my family circle and myself, I precisely concluded my biography with the necessary words, "The End". Little did I know, it was just the beginning.

Often times in life we fail to see the early correlations between the patterns formed in our lives and the person we become. Life causes us to detour and take unlikely turns. Nevertheless, our destinies are shaped by early patterns. Some people tend to remember every aspect of their childhood. I, however, find it very difficult to remember many past childhood events for one reason or another. I do remember some good memories. Maybe I chose to selectively block out some of the not so good memories. Most people remember more.

I was a very creative child. I enjoyed writing, poetry, dancing, and listening to records on our family's large console stereo. It was a brown piece of furniture with a red power light at the bottom. I just knew that I could see my favorite artists performing inside it if I pressed my eyes against the red light hard enough.

Writing always came easy for me. I guess you could say that I was destined to put pen to paper. There is something about memorializing the many issues of life. Life's issues and struggles have made some ugly scars. We all come to a point in life where we have to realistically deal with the hand we have been dealt. Dealing with the hand that we have been dealt is like "dancing" through life. So often we dance with partners. Sometimes we must dance with the scars. I have experienced them both. Here's my story.

1. IN THE BEGINNING

I was always a very precocious child. Older people would refer to me as having "an old spirit" I really can't say why that was the case. I only know that I always felt as though I did not fit in my age group or with my peers. *Have you ever felt as though you were looking at life from the outside in? You can see life occurring, but it is as though you are a spectator.*

I have always been a thinker. I like to process things and analyze things, probably to a fault. I like to know the "why"of things and the background behind things. This is probably why I found it difficult to cheat off of someone's paper in grade school. I was too busy trying to figure out "how"they got the answer that they had instead of taking their answer and running with it.

More than anything, I have always LOVED to dance. While growing up, I was convinced that I was going to be the next Judith Jamison. Judith was a dancer and choreographer with the Alvin Ailey Dance Theater. She was tall, flowing, and full of grace. Her body was very gazelle-like. I had a poster of her on my bedroom wall showing her leaping ever so confidently into the air. I was convinced that I was going to be a famous dancer. I did not have her height, but I was working on the poise and the grace.

My dance portfolio included studies at Miss Young's School of Dance and Miss Donna's School of Dance. I studied ballet, tap, baton, and modern dance. *I was sure to excel in at least one of these.*

Miss Young was stern and very professional. She always wore her wavy hair pulled back. Her studio was on the Westside of Charlotte. I remember having to walk up a long flight of metal stairs on the outside of her building to get to her studio. Dance rehearsal was a weekly Saturday morning highlight for me. *Plié and point, plié and point, raise the arm, then out to the side.* After rehearsal, I would clank, clank, clank back down the metal stairs to walk to the take-out chicken restaurant which was next door until my ride came to pick me up. There was no sitting area inside of the restaurant. The food had to be ordered at the counter and then taken out. Boy did they have good fried chicken and fried fish!

I later started a Community Dance Group in my neighborhood when I was in Junior High School. There were four or five of us. We would dance at different community centers and other local events. A neighbor by the name of Miss Pat would sometimes let us rehearse in her basement. She was the only house in the neighborhood (that I was aware of) that had a basement. It was our private neighborhood dance studio. By the time I got to high school, I helped to start a dance group there as well. I also danced with a group in college called the "Opeyo! Dancers" *Opeyo is Swahili for "beyond the horizon"* In my mind, New York City, here I come!

DANCE has been a part of my entire life. However, once I developed a relationship with the Lord, I discovered a spiritual connection with God through the experience of sacred dance. It's almost like an outerbody experience. No one else exists but me and Him. There is a "time to dance" I believe that something powerful happens when we dance for the Lord.

We become joyful — "You have turned my mourning into dancing." (Psalm 30:11)

We become worshipful — "Let them praise His name with dancing." (Psalm 149:3)

We demonstrate celebration — "Praise Him with timbrel and dancing." (Psalm 150:4)

"They send forth their little ones like a flock and their children dance." (Job 21:11)

"When Jephthah came to his house at Mizpah, there was his daughter, coming out to meet him with timbrels and dancing." (Judges 11:34)

"Then Miriam the prophetess, the sister of Aaron, took the timbrel in her hand; and all the women went out after her with timbrels and with dances." (Exodus 15:20)

"Then David danced before the Lord with all his might; and David was wearing a linen ephod." (2 Samuel 6:14)

We are the product of our experiences. Lord, I offer up dance to You.

2. DANCING WITH DISTRACTIONS, DISTORTIONS, AND DECEIT

I've always liked boys. Not boy crazy, but I was never confused about "me Jane, him Tarzan." The sad part is, I didn't read the life script beforehand to know that boys are never quite that simple. That's probably why I experienced a number of failed relationships particularly after the passing of my father.

My father passed when I was around fourteen years old. I was a "daddy's girl." I recall him cooking me breakfast each morning, placing it on a plate, and putting it on the table for me to come eat.

I recall when I was elementary age, riding with my dad each Monday to take my sister to orchestra rehearsal. While she was inside the school in rehearsal, he and I would ride to KFC and order my favorite meal (one chicken leg, coleslaw, and mashed potatoes and gravy). We would sit in the car and eat it while we waited on her. Now those were the good ole days for real! I miss those special moments with my dad. He always made me feel special.

I never understood the specifics surrounding his death because it was one of those things you just did not talk about. During those years, people just did not talk about death and dying. There was little help for those dealing with death. The person you loved was here today and then they were gone. You had a funeral, and that was it.

As a young teenager, that was very confusing for me. I wanted answers. I needed answers. My last memory of my father was when I visited him in the hospital. He was weak, but in good spirits. I was told that he had an aneurysm. At that time, I had no idea what that meant. I have come to learn that it is the rupture of a blood vessel wall in the brain cavity. That one significant event, I believe, was the turning point in my life.

See it was at that point, as much of a cliché as it may be, that I began to 'look for love in all the wrong places.' In fact, that is an understatement.

My Distraction - David Morgan (names are changed to protect the innocent).

He was a couple of years older than me. I was an up and coming freshman in high school and he was a senior. He was protective, funny, and had a good heart. We crossed the line, and boom, I was pregnant. I was fifteen years old and it was shortly after my father had died.

Being very naïve, I really didn't understand what was going on with my body. We decided to tell my mother together. Fireworks! She was one angry black woman!

My mother was a very educated and respected woman in our community. She had served with the National Council of Negro Women; she was on leadership boards in the church; she was an educator and a mentor to numerous students, and she played a significant role in her sorority, Sigma Gamma Rho. She did not receive the news of my pregnancy well.

The Distortion

Days after we shared our dilemma with her, I recall being driven to Atlanta by my mom and her girlfriend to a clinic to have the abortion. This was around 1978. I was so far along in the pregnancy (not sure how many weeks because it didn't mean anything to me at the time) that it was not even legal to have the abortion in North Carolina.

We drove to Atlanta in silence. No one asked any questions. No one asked me how I felt. No one asked if I understood what was getting ready to happen. Nothing.

We arrived at a hospital and they essentially induced my labor. I walked the halls for hours in pain until it was time.

The doctor very callously performed a partial birth abortion. In other words, he delivered a dead baby that he killed in utero. (Partial birth abortions were declared illegal in the United States in 2003 and the Partial Birth Abortion Ban Act was upheld in 2007.)

We drove back to Charlotte. No one said a word about it. EVER!

I recall going back to school on that Monday. I was bleeding heavily. I didn't understand why.

Notice the following facts about teen pregnancy according to dosomething.org:

- 3 in 10 American teen girls will get pregnant at least once before age 20. That's nearly 750,000 teen pregnancies every year.
- Parenthood is the leading reason that teen girls drop out of school. More than half of teen mothers never graduate from high school.
- Less than 2 percent of teen moms earn a college degree by age 30.
- About a quarter of teen moms have a second child within 24 months of their first baby.
- The United States has one of the highest teen pregnancy rates in the western industrialized world.
- 8 out of 10 teen dads don't marry the mother of their child.

- Almost 50 percent of teens have never considered how a pregnancy would affect their lives.

The Deceit

It's interesting how we learn early in life to "pretend" to be something and someone that we are not. We can appear so confident on the outside and be so full of shame on the inside.

I remember as a young girl learning what it meant to be an imposter and believing that I had found a word that defined who I was. Everyone saw me as this innocent, sweet, bright young girl. Teachers loved me. My friends' parents loved me. And I still remained the apple of my mother's eye. Sometimes a person can even fool herself into believing that she really is great and wonderful. I sure did.

My mom essentially kicked David to the curb. He was not good enough for her daughter anyway, she felt. Don't get me wrong. I loved my mom very much, but this was a very confusing time for me. I didn't understand why. Why him? Why me? Why the abortion? Why that way?

Lord, prepare me to be a sanctuary
Pure and holy, tried and true
With thanksgiving, I'll be a living
Sanctuary for You

It is You, Lord
Who came to save
The heart and soul
Of every man
It is You Lord
who knows my weakness
Who gives me strength,
With Thine own hand.

Lord prepare me to be a sanctuary
Pure and Holy, tried and true
With thanksgiving I'll be a living
Sanctuary for You

Lead me on, Lord
From temptation
Purify me
From within
Fill my heart with
Your Holy Spirit
Take away all my sin

Lord prepare me to be a sanctuary
Pure and holy, tried and true
With thanksgiving, I'll be a living
Sanctuary for You

3. FRESH WIND... I THINK!

I graduated from high school with advanced level classes and I proceeded on to college at the University of North Carolina at Greensboro. I was going to be a dancer on Broadway and open my own studio. I could finally put the past behind me...I thought, and move on to another chapter of my life. New season! Great expectations! Fresh wind!

David was a distant memory. Little did I know, there would be other David types. Over time, one flaw would surface in one of my male friends, and then another flaw. Time to move on to another "David."

David #2 was seven years older than I. I was 18. He was 25. I was a freshman in college. He was a college graduate who had been in the armed services. He wanted a long-term committed relationship: *Marriage. Home. Cooking and cleaning. Was he kidding me?* I wanted to have a good time. I was mature and at the same time immature. *Little girl, sit down somewhere!*

That didn't last very long. He was a man. I was a girl. *Call in the next group of Davids, please.* I continued to make surface choices. If he looked good, or sounded good, he was the flavor of the month. It took a while for this to get old. Ignorance *is* bliss.

There is a certain amount of naivety that comes with our youthfulness. If we are fortunate, we will grow out of it. But one's college and young adult years can be very scarring.

For me, college introduced me to light drinking—mostly beer. That's what a lot of college kids do. I had been a "good girl" for the most part, so this was new, exciting, and oh, so grown! At the time, *Mickey* Beer was the big thing. They were packaged in small green bottles. As I think back, they really had an awful taste to them. But it was my drink of choice.

I do not recall the specifics of "that" night. There must have been some type of party or something, but I definitely had been drinking. Since I was not a drinker, it didn't take much for me to pass out. Somehow, I got back to my room in North Spencer Dorm. There was a senior guy who I was familiar with who was in the room too. He was a big guy compared to most. He had a beard and wore glasses. I can still see his frame in my mind. I really don't recall why he was in my room or if other people were in my room. I just know that I was very aware that he was there, and it was as if I was having an out of body experience. I was lying on my bed.

He started to unfasten my pants. My body was limp as though I had no control over it at all, and it was as if my voice had been muted. Nothing came out. He pulled my pants down. He unzipped his pants, and he got on top of me. I felt as though I was suffocating because of his weight. After only a few moments, he was done. He got up and he left. At some point during the night, I attempted to pull myself together and sort out in my brain whether I was having a nightmare or not. It was real. The residue of him remained. This man had raped me! I NEVER TOLD A SOUL!

God's Grace

The Lord has a unique way of carrying us through the vicissitudes of life. The fascinating thing about life and the power of our minds is that we have the ability to push events aside in our mind and move on to the next life event. Somehow though, they seem to always creep back in. *So many scars, but still dancing.*

I have learned that this is why having a genuine relationship with the Lord is so important. You can tell Him what you're too afraid or ashamed to tell anyone else. He renews us, refreshes us, and He gives us the strength to keep on moving in the midst of life events. It took me a while to fully understand this. People can tell you how something works, but there are some things that don't hit home until you experience them for yourself. I have had to experience a lot of things for myself for this to resonate with me. Someone once said, "that which does not kill you, must make you stronger." Well, I should be able to roll a boulder over!

This is the kind of tenacity that makes the Apostle Paul such an interesting character. He started out as a persecutor of the church. Then he was converted on the road to Damascus. He was struck down by a bolt of light and temporarily blinded. *Now that ought to get your attention.* He was later beaten, abused, shipwrecked and stoned. Nevertheless, he eventually came to a point in his life when he realized that he had to rely upon the grace of God.

Grace is God's unmerited favor. It is what He gives us in spite of us and in spite of what we have done, what we have said, and how we have behaved. It is like a wind blowing over us that protects us from harm and danger. It's like a divine safety net that propels us back into the air again.

Because of the surpassing greatness of the revelations, for this reason, to keep me from exalting myself, there was given me a thorn in the flesh, a messenger of Satan to torment me—to keep me from exalting myself!

Concerning this I implored the Lord three times that

it might leave me.

And He has said to me, "My grace is sufficient for you, for power is perfected in weakness." Most gladly, therefore, I will rather boast about my weaknesses, so that the power of Christ may dwell in me.

Therefore I am well content with weaknesses, with insults, with distresses, with persecutions, with difficulties, for Christ's sake; for when I am weak, then I am strong. (2 Corinthians 12:7-10)

4. IT'S ABOUT FAITH

After my first year of college, I transferred to the University of North Carolina at Chapel Hill. Becoming a dancer was a nice dream, but let's face it, I was going to need a real job in the real world. Besides, the *right* David was a student at Chapel Hill. My high school crush would finally bring us together to live happily ever after. *Somebody should have told this David my plans for our lives. He forgot to read the script. His story had a different ending.*

After college, I determined to live my life and make my mark by being a part of committees, boards, and all the other "in" stuff. I was young, black, educated, attractive, and handling my business. And my *scars* were perfectly covered.

Yet, there still seemed to be something missing. A void. An emptiness. Of course I attended church—the one that all the buppies attended. (That's a black yuppie or upwardly mobile person, for those who are unaware.) I attended the buppie church so that I could definitely increase my chances of connecting with someone who could open a door or share an opportunity. Life seemed good, at least I thought, but there was *still* something left out. I just couldn't put my finger on it.

I believe we do our current generation a grave disservice. We tell them to get an education (which they do need), strive, compete, excel and climb the ladder. There is nothing wrong with all of that, however, too little focus is put on who they are as individuals. What they should stand for. The importance of integrity, character, and internal fortitude.

Have you ever wanted something, and you didn't know what it was? All you know is that you want *something*. I don't mean a choice between a hamburger and a taco. No something much deeper than that. Something more meaningful than that. Something more fulfilling than that. That is why prayer is so important. At times, I would pray and it helps me to gain a clearer focus on my perspective. When my focus becomes fine-tuned, then I am in a better position to believe God for what He has put in my heart and in my spirit. That is when I am able to activate my faith to believe in that which I do not see and I cannot articulate.

Faith came into play regarding my desire to get pregnant. That's right! I actually got to a place where I wanted to be pregnant. That was truly an act of God!

But life has a funny way of throwing you curve balls. It

all came together for me after becoming an adult. I was told for a long time that I would not be able to get pregnant. Of course, this took me back to the abortion in my past as well as the thought that God was punishing me. God does not do that, but that was where my mind went and I was okay with that. I felt like it was His right to do that if He decided to do so. I was not mad at Him. I simply believed if you do something bad, God punishes you and you just reap the consequences. You get what you deserve. But it is not quite that simple.

After meeting and marrying my husband, everything changed. For so long, I had told myself that I did not want to have a child. At least that is what I *said*.

Like many women, I believe that a part of me wanted a child, but I had convinced myself otherwise to sort of soften the blow of my probably not being able to have a child. But when I met Michael L. Henderson, Sr., the script was flipped. I thought to myself, this is someone I might be able to do this with. *Grin. Blush.* He was not just good-looking, he was also respectful, smart, spiritual, and not afraid to take the lead as the man.

After we met, we talked about children and we talked about children and talked about it some more. We both said that we did not want children. I really thought I was being true to myself because I did not believe that God would even allow me to have a child. But deep down, it was not what I felt. As you can imagine, my true feelings eventually began to surface.

I began to say, "I do want this." He would say, "Well, I don't want this." After a few years, he began to say, "I do want this," and then it didn't happen.

By the time, we were five years into our marriage, we had tried various natural avenues to conceive. I recall using a menstrual cycle wheel. It was a spiral cardboard wheel. The dates on the wheel had to be lined up with the first date of your menstrual cycle. The wheel would show the dates that you were most likely to conceive. That didn't work either. The one thing I knew was what God had told me. I knew we were supposed to have a child. I didn't know how that would come about, but I knew that it was part of my destiny.

5. MORE FAITH

Honestly, our faith had begun to waver. We went to an adoption agency with the hope of starting a family. We quickly realized that, in order to go through the adoption process, it would require numerous weekends of training and lots of dedicated time that we, quite frankly, did not have at that point. With our hectic ministry lives, we just did not have the time to make it all come together. We were genuinely trying to stay open to how God wanted to move in this situation. Things just were not working out.

After the adoption attempt, there seemed to be even more wind taken out of our sail. My husband said, "This is not meant to happen. We need to let this dream die." He did not mean any harm. He simply saw the emotional toll that it was taking and it just did not seem to be worth it. However, something on the inside of me just could not and would not let the dream die.

The great Harlem Renaissance poet, Langston Hughes, penned the now famous poem,

Harlem

What happens to a dream deferred?

Does it dry up?

Like a raisin in the sun?

Or fester like a sore—

And then run?

Does it stink like rotten meat?

Or crust and sugar over—

Like a syrupy sweet?

Maybe it just sags

Like a heavy load.

Or does it explode?

I was convinced that there was a glimmer of hope. I continued to pray. I used to keep a prayer journal and every day I asked the Lord to honor my prayer. Here are some of those entries from my prayer journal:

April 12, 2002 – Lord, bless the fruit of my womb.

April 24, 2002 – Lord, I still believe that You have called me to give birth to a healthy child. I call my child into existence.

May 6, 2002 – Have Your way in my life, in my womb. Thank You in advance for conception, good pregnancy, safe delivery, healthy baby.

June 1, 2002 – Pastors Leon & Carol Threatt prayed for my womb and me today. They told me to name my child, call him/her by name everyday and then to believe God for the manifestation.

June 28, 2002 – Open my womb, Lord. Thank You in advance that in Your perfect timing, I will conceive.

August 7, 2002 – I believe You, Lord, for a miracle baby.

September 5, 2002 – It is Day 30 and no menstrual cycle. Although the pregnancy test was negative, I still positively believe You for conception in my womb. I believe and receive it!

I consistently wrote in my journal every day. I was trusting and believing in God for more faith.

One day, I happened to run into an old friend from college. We were the same age—Thirty-nine years old. She told me about her new daughter and shared with me about a book entitled *Supernatural Childbirth* by Jackie Mize. My friend had discovered the book, read the book, and was convinced that it had helped to take her faith to another level. My husband thought I was crazy. *What did I have to lose?*

The book uniquely deals with activating one's faith in

order to believe God for what seems like the impossible. It was so inspiring to read about all the women in the Bible who were once barren but had their wombs opened by God: women like Sarah, Rebekah, Leah, Rachel, Hannah, Manoah's wife (Samson's mother), the Shunammite woman, and Elisabeth, (mother of John the Baptist). Reading the book was absolutely revolutionary for me because I had not thought about those women and their plights. When I started reading about the different stories and different women, my reaction was, "Wow, God did that!"

My favorite biblical character is Hannah. Her story is found in the book of I Samuel chapter one. Hannah was married to a man named Elkanah. (His other wife was Peninnah. That storyline brings its own drama with it). Anyway, Peninnah had children but Hannah was barren. Like me, Hannah desperately wanted a child. Her husband loved her in spite of her barrenness which was very unusual for that period of time. Barrenness was frowned upon in biblical times. One day Hannah decided to make a trip to Shiloh to the tabernacle of God to see Eli the priest. *There's something about being in the place of God when you are in a state of desperation.* Hannah prayed to God and wept bitterly. She even made a deal with God. She vowed to Him that if He would give her a son, she would give the son back to Him. *Have you ever made a deal with God? God, if You will just do THIS, I will do*

THAT! Please God! Just this once. I promise I'll hold up my end of the bargain.

In Hannah's great desperation, she cried out to the Lord for a child. Eli the priest thought she was drunk. Hannah explained to him that she wasn't drunk, just oppressed in her spirit. For some reason, it appears from Eli's reaction, that he is satisfied with her answer. He tells Hannah, "Go in peace; and may the God of Israel grant your petition that you have asked of Him."

After Eli spoke this to Hannah, it was as if there was a release in her spirit that allowed her to "let it go"because she was no longer downcast. *There have been times when I simply had to cry it out, shout it out, or dance it out in order to get a release.* Well, the rest is history. Hannah worshiped the Lord, went back home, got with her husband Elkanah and *bam*, she was pregnant! The Lord had answered her desperate cry.

Hannah's story was very encouraging to me. I was able to get a release in my spirit about my heart's desire and let go without giving up my desire. Hebrews chapter eleven verse one states, *"Faith is the confidence that what we hope for will actually happen; it gives us assurance about things we cannot see"*(New Living Translation). **What a dance of faith.**

6. IT'S WORTH THE WAIT

By early 2003, I found myself taking a pregnancy test every time I had a stomachache. *I'm sure I had become an unsuspecting stockholder in Clearblue pregnancy tests.* April 12, 2003, is the date that I will always remember. We were hosting our first Women's Conference at the church. One of the speakers was Rev. Renee Cole from Maryland. I had met her a time or two before but we didn't have a close relationship. I admired her ministry from afar. She spoke on that Friday night and again on Saturday morning. At the end of her message on Saturday morning, she put her hand on my stomach and prophetically spoke, "out of your womb you will birth forth..." I was shocked. Amazed. Stunned. Mesmerized. Blown away. Not because it was what I wanted to hear. It was an amazing confirmation. See, I had taken my last Clearblue on the previous evening, and this time Clearblue **was** blue. *Hal-le-lujah! Hallelujah, hallelujah!*

There was NO way she could have known. I had told no one. I was waiting to share it the perfect way. After composing myself, I went back to my house after the conference concluded. It just so happened that my sister-in-law, Josephine, was one of the conference speakers. She was in town staying with us. Also my mother-in-law was in town along with another sister-in-law, Lolita. It was a family affair.

We were all at our home, eating, fellowshipping and reflecting on the conference. We were having a great time. I was ready to burst! I finally decided that I could not take it any longer. I called my husband upstairs and he reluctantly followed me. *I had always imagined how I would tell my husband that I was pregnant. Would I take him to dinner and wrap the test in a small box? Would I ask him to guess my secret? Would I give him a card with a baby's footprint inside?* No time for all that. I exclaimed, "Here, look at this!" I handed him the carefully wrapped Clearblue test. As Celie in the movie *The Color Purple* did, I then stood back to watch his reaction. He took the test from my hand and said "Huh? What's this? What's that line? What does this mean?" I paused for a moment and then said, "This means I am pregnant!" He looked bewildered and scared. It was a sight to see. Then he said, "Are you sure? Is this accurate? We need a blood test." I'm convinced he was in shock. *Could it be that the little book that he smirked at me for reading, actually helped to increase my faith? Was it possible that my prayers had been heard and honored by God? Could it be? Yes, man of God, it is so!*

7. THE GOOD LIFE

We proceeded downstairs where we still had a house full of guests. Of course we had to share our happy news with them. What were the chances that so many family members would be at our home at a time like this?

As we cleared our throats, we said, "Can we get everyone's attention. We have an announcement to make." Everyone looked puzzled, wondering what required such grandstanding. Without any pomp or circumstance, we announced, "We are going to have a baby!" *What a relief to get that out.* Everyone looked amazed. We were all ecstatic!

One of our church members who was a nurse advised me not to share the news publicly until I was at least twelve weeks along. I agreed. I knew that the early stages of pregnancy could be very volatile and making a premature announcement could be devastating. In addition, I was forty years old. It was definitely a high-risk pregnancy.

My husband on the other hand seemed to be happier than I. After only a few weeks, he could not hold it anymore. He announced to our church that we had news to share but we could not tell them what it was at that time. *Well, anyone with a small amount of insight could figure out that maybe he was referring to my being pregnant.* The cat was out of the bag in no time. It felt good to share our happy news.

I think when you continuously pray for something and it finally comes to pass, it can be a little overwhelming. *"Ask and it will be given to you; seek and you will find; knock and it will be opened to you"(Matthew 7:7).* It seemed as though it had been such a long journey to get to this point in time. It was exciting, fulfilling, and a bit frightening, all at the same time. The saddest part though was that my mother was not able to experience the joy of my pregnancy with me. My mother passed away on January 26, 1999, nine months before we started New Beginnings Community Church. My mother and I were very close. We were probably too close. My husband used to say that our relationship was enmeshed. *What did he know?* I will admit that our relationship probably had traces of dysfunction throughout it. We would talk on the phone several times a day. I knew way too much about her life and she knew way too little about mine. I would do anything for her and vice versa. She was my mother and my best friend. So here I am at this pinnacle in my womanhood and the one person who I could count on to celebrate this incredible joy with me was gone. *Ain't life strange!*

I enjoyed my pregnancy. Special seating. Special parking. Being able to put my feet up when needed. Watching my belly grow. Now that's the good life! I didn't have a lot of cravings during that time. Cooked liver was one of my cravings. Hotdogs was the other. It's difficult to find a fast food restaurant that serves hotdogs. I recall having a really bad craving for a hotdog one evening. I called several fast food restaurants to inquire about hotdogs on their menu. It was very discouraging. Then I located a Hardee's, which was about fifteen minutes from where we lived. It was close to Indian Trail, NC. My husband drove me there to satisfy my late night craving only to arrive moments before their closing. So as not to miss the opportunity to fulfill my ever-increasing craving, I jumped out of the car and ran over to the drive-through window and told the attendant that it was an emergency. "I HAVE to have a hotdog," I exclaimed! Mission accomplished! Oh, the things that pregnant women do.

8. AN UPHILL BATTLE

After a few months into my pregnancy, I started swelling quite a bit. My feet. My hands. Even my face. I felt like a brown Pillsbury Doughboy. I assumed that this was normal. I did have a human being growing on the inside of me. We were so excited about going to get the ultrasound at sixteen weeks. We would finally find out the sex of our baby. The nurse took us back to the examining room. The doctor came in and rubbed gel on my belly. He then took an instrument that looked like a showerhead and rotated it across my belly. After a few moments he said, "See that little thing there? That means it's a boy." We were elated. They gave us pictures of the ultrasound that I immediately blew up and framed. It was another happy day.

By week twenty-four, I was extremely tired, swollen, and had an excruciating headache that would not go away. I called my obstetrician's office. They informed the doctor on call and they called in a prescription for me. I filled the prescription and started on the medication but it seemed to be no help at all. I needed relief and I needed it bad. By the end of that week, we were preparing to fly to St. Thomas, Virgin Islands for a vacation. Great idea. Wrong time. My headache had not gotten any better and the thought of a four plus hour flight was not making it any better. We arrived in St. Thomas. Just as I had suspected, I was miserable. My headache was worse. Nothing seemed to help. It was the longest three days of my life.

After suffering through the trip, I made it back without my head exploding. Fortunately that Monday was a holiday so I was able to rest. I stayed in the bed all day long. On Tuesday, I managed to get up, go to work and appeared to function like a normal person. Fortunately my doctor's appointment was after work that day. I made it through the day and to my regular monthly appointment. When I arrived, they proceeded through the normal routine of weighing me and taking my blood pressure. After getting my blood pressure reading, my doctor came in and shared that my blood pressure was extremely high. It was 200 over 106. He wanted me to go straight to the hospital. *What are you talking about? My blood pressure has never been an issue before. I told you guys that the pain in my head felt like a missile flying around inside of it.*

I don't think I fully understood the severity of my situation. Instead of going straight to the hospital, I decided to go home and get my husband. I knew that if I needed to stay at the hospital, I would need an overnight bag. Besides, the pain in my head had been ricocheting for over a week. Certainly, one more hour would not make that much of a difference.

By the grace of God, I made it home. I tried to explain to my husband what was going on to the best of my ability. I don't think I did a good job. I had no idea what was going on myself. I packed my bag and we headed to the hospital. It was Tuesday. After arriving, I was admitted on the maternity floor. *Can somebody tell me what is going on?*

After getting settled into my hospital room, I was finally told that I was experiencing what is called preeclampsia. Preeclampsia is a form of toxemia (which is a type of blood poisoning). Usually it causes hypertension (high blood pressure) and fluid retention (remember the brown Pillsbury doughboy?) It still did not make sense to me. I was given medication for my blood pressure. I started charting my blood pressure to see if it was going down. It was slowly moving down but not to a normal level. Of course, my nerves were shot by this point so that did not help my blood pressure at all. *Lord, hide me in Your secret pavilion.*

My headache had stopped. *Praise the Name of the Lord.*

There was talk amongst the hospital doctors and my doctor that I might have to stay in the hospital for the remainder of my pregnancy term. *Are you crazy? I'm twenty-five weeks along.* Two days went by. On the morning of the third day, my headache returned. I immediately informed the on-duty nurse that my head was hurting again. I was told to lie on my left side. That did not help. Nurses and doctors and doctors and nurses.

There was a lot of looking at my medical chart along with whispers and people moving really fast. By late afternoon, I was told that I would have to have an emergency cesarean section. The procedure is commonly known as a C-section and it entails the cutting through the walls of the abdomen and uterus in order to remove the fetus. A neonatal specialist came in my hospital room to inform me that my situation was very critical and that I could lose the baby. He also said that the baby could be born with multiple complications. A nurse came in to give me a shot that would help to strengthen the baby's lungs. They continued to prep me for surgery. In the meantime, I'm trying to wrap my mind around all that was happening. *I'm baffled. I'm confused. I'm scared. My faith is waning.*

9. DANCING WITH THE SCARS

My husband was at the hospital during this time. Neither of us had any idea that it would be an all day ordeal. He appeared steady and strong which was comforting for me. Our lives were getting ready to change forever. He immediately began to pray.

This is the confidence that we have before Him, that if we ask anything according to His will, He hears us. And if we know that He hears us in whatever we ask, we know that we have the requests which we have asked from Him. (2 John 5:14-15)

I do not know what my husband prayed that night. I only know that I needed prayer and I needed it badly. They finally wheeled me into the operating area. The technician in the operating room explained to me the process of an epidural. An epidural is an anesthesia injected into the spine, commonly used with pregnant women to numb the abdominal area and below in preparation for childbirth. The technician told me that it was important that I remain extremely still during the insertion because if there is any movement, it could easily cause paralysis since the anesthetic is being injected into the lumbar area of the spine. *I thought to myself, a piece of cake, lady! Once I get around the fact that I am in a cold, sterile room with total strangers preparing for an emergency C-section while at twenty-five weeks of gestation, I should have no problem at all!*

The epidural insertion went well. After they were assured that I had no sense of feeling in my lower extremities, they helped me lay down on the operating table. At some point, my husband was allowed into the operating area. There was a woman over my head who was talking to me the entire time. I don't know who she was or what her official role was, but she kept asking me if I was okay. She told me that everything was going to be okay. She told me that I was doing a great job. *Remember the television show, "Touched By An Angel" It premiered in 1994. It was about an earthly angel who helped to communicate messages from God to people to help them and guide them through various life issues.* I really believe that this woman was my angel. She kept me calm throughout the entire surgery and she talked to me as though she knew me. I asked about her days later. No one knew who I was talking about.

I don't recall a lot about the surgery. I felt pressure around my stomach at one point. I really believe that it was my internal organs that my doctor was placing on top of me in order to get the baby out. *Childbirth is no joke!* I had no idea that I had just delivered a one pound one ounce baby. He was 483 grams. Once the surgery was over, I was still very groggy. They rolled me back to my room with a lot of IVs attached. Everything was a blur. Was I a mother? It was September 5, 2003.

Deep Wounds

The next day was very dark—not just the room, but also my spirit. I felt bad. I looked bad. I had a catheter attached to me. No one was there. I was slipping into a depression. *Do you blame me? I felt like my life was being sucked into a black hole.*

I laid there in my hospital bed with a constant beeping from the IV machine. It was slowly and methodically administering some type of solution into my body to prevent seizures. The sound was as aggravating as a ticking clock. *Drip. Drip. Drip. I get it! They want me to lose my mind.*

I finally decided to push the call button on the bed. The nurse at the station came in. I did not really want anything. I simply needed someone there. She sat beside my bed and talked with me and tried to make me laugh. I do not remember the conversation, but I do recall that she was very warm and comforting. *Could it be another angel?*

She finally had to get back to work. Shortly after that, a hospital aide came in and told me that she was there to give me my bath. *My what?* She said she was directed to give me a sponge bath from my bed and to change the sheets underneath me. Of course I thought she was kidding. I had never had this done before. Now, I felt like an elderly person in a convalescent home.

She opened the curtains to let some light in. I had no idea that the sun was shining as brightly as it was. It was bright, crisp, and almost uplifting. We made it through the bath. The hospital aide proceeded with the bathing as though she had done it hundreds of times. I think she just wanted to get it over with. Lord knows *I* really wanted to get it over with.

By midday, the nurse on duty asked me if I wanted to see my baby. *My baby? I have a baby? I am a mother? Will he know who I am? We had decided months earlier to call him MJ.* I finally conceded and I was wheeled down to the neonatal intensive care unit (NICU). We got to the two large doors and had to wait to be beeped in. After entering, I immediately heard lots of beeping. I was told to wash my hands for at least two minutes prior to entering the floor area. By this time, my mind was racing. This was all very new and different. When I was pregnant, I toured the hospital like most moms-to-be did, but I did not recall the NICU on the tour. In fact, I recall the tour guide whisking my group pass the NICU hallway and mumbling something about us not having to worry about that area. We proceeded into the floor area of the NICU. It was unusually dim. There were lots of isolettes (a type of incubator) with babies in them. Various families were huddled in various corners of the floor. Everyone looked serious.

We walked towards the back of the unit and approached the isolette with my baby. When I looked inside, I was not prepared for what I saw. No one would be. He was tiny. There were tubes coming out of every area of his body. There was lots of beeping. I noticed a tube down his throat that was taped to his mouth. His diaper looked as though it could have fit a child's doll. He couldn't be touched. His skin was translucent. *Lord, this is not what I prayed for!*

Scarred For Life

At that moment it hit me that my life would never be the same again. I was scarred. Deeply scarred. And it was clear that, for the rest of my life, I would be *dancing with the scars.*

MJ had a number of medical challenges due to his prematurity including retinopathy of prematurity (ROP), broncho-pulmonary dysplasia, gastroesophageal reflux, pulmonary hemorrhage, respiratory distress syndrome and hypotension. He required total parenteral nutrition support

(TPN) as well as gastronomy feeds. He also contracted pneumonia and a wound infection on his left heel. The days and weeks and months to come were a blur. Every day that MJ was in the NICU became more and more exhausting. The doctors recited their usual negative mantras about all the worse case possibilities. *Doctors have an uncanny ability to leave you with no hope at the expense of leaving you with false hope.* Baby MJ's life was touch and go for months. There were numerous scares with the ventilator. When they have to turn the ventilator support up very high, they notify you because they assume that the patient will soon be brain dead. There were infections, setbacks, and lots and lots of beeping. It was all so overwhelming.

Has the Lord rejected me forever? Will He never again be kind to me? Is His unfailing love gone forever? Have His promises permanently failed? Has God forgotten to be gracious? (Psalm 77:7-9, New Living Translation)

There was one bright spot after about three months of anxiety. It was called Kangaroo Care. Nurse Laura, another true angel, introduced me to it. Kangaroo Care is a bonding technique that allows a parent to carefully hold her baby next to her bare skin so that there is skin-to-skin contact. It is often used with pre-term babies. Somehow the skin-to-skin contact helps to stabilize the baby's body temperature.

I did not fully understand it then. I only knew that it was a lifesaver at a time when I needed one. Getting MJ out of the isolette was a major deal. One tube had to be disconnected and then another one. The transfer to my arms had to be quick. I would sit in the rocker beside his isolette and rock him on my chest for as long as I could.

Hush little baby, don't say a word,
Mama's gonna buy you a mockingbird,
If that mocking bird don't sing,
Mama's gonna buy you a diamond ring,
If that diamond ring won't shine,
Hush little baby don't you mind,
Cuz if that diamond ring don't shine,
Mama's gonna love you 'til the end of time,
I'm always gonna love you 'til the end of time.
(Author Unknown)

I *almost* forgot that the conditions were not normal. When my time was up, letting him go was the hardest thing to do. It was as though someone was ripping a part of me from my soul. *I would learn to dance and dance and dance…with the scars.*

10. TWO ARE BETTER THAN ONE

When you first get married, everyone tells you that "everyday will not be a bed of roses" I don't know what that really means, but I do know that the crucibles of life can put an incredible amount of strain on any relationship. Jesus said, "Here on earth you will have many trials and sorrows" (John 16:33 NLT). In other words, it is to be expected to have to go through hard times, difficult times, challenging times, and valley times. *I'm sorry but that does not make me feel any better at all!*

I recall one of MJ's doctors saying to me and my husband that he was surprised that we were still together after all that we had gone through with MJ's prematurity. *Doc, are you kidding me?* He was truly baffled that we still had a viable relationship and were supportive of one another. What the doctor did not know was that there was a "B" clause to verse thirty-three of John 16. It states, "But take heart, because I have overcome the world." *Now THAT does make me feel better!*

There is no way that my husband and I could have gotten through the stress and strain of all that we were going through without making a conscious and determined decision to grab hold to Someone much greater than ourselves. The authenticity of our relationship with the Lord was tested for sure. See there was no way for us to *really* know that God was a "present help" unless we needed him "presently." Even though we did not sit down with one another and discuss the theological constructs of God's attributes within the context of our medical and psychological dilemma, we both knew within ourselves that **Jesus was in the midst of our trial**!

During that season, life may have seemed crazy, but we knew that Jesus was right there! Life may have seemed unbearable, but we knew that Jesus was right there! Life may have seemed overwhelming, but we knew that Jesus was right there! Life may have seemed unfair, but we knew that Jesus was right there!

A person standing alone can be attacked and defeated, but two can stand back-to-back and conquer. Three are even better, for a triple-braided cord is not easily broken. (Eccl 4:12, NLT)

We did not have time to point fingers or find someone

to blame. It was so important for us to keep the main thing the main thing so that God could be glorified through all that was occurring. Was it easy? Of course not!

We dealt with the reality of our experience differently. For me, it was therapeutic to be at the hospital every time that the neonatal intensive care unit was open for visitors. I knew the name of every doctor, nurse, technician and cleaning staff that worked on that floor. It was not something that I wanted to do. It was something that I "had" to do. And as a mother, the maternal bond that was formed inside of me, compelled me to camp out as often as possible on the sixth floor of the hospital.

On the other hand, my husband dealt with the reality of our experience in another way. He went to the hospital as much as he could, but the pain of seeing his only son fighting for his life while knowing that he could physically do nothing to help him was simply too much to bear. It was more therapeutic for him to research every piece of information on prematurity that there was. He ordered every book, read every online articles, and goggled every term that was thrown at us from the doctors. *I think he's an expert on the subject by now.*

The television host and psychologist, *Dr. Phil*, often says, "how's that working for you?" Well it worked just fine for us. I respected my husband's way of dealing and he respected mine. Too often, we want others to experience what we feel in the same way that we feel and that is totally unrealistic. Fortunately for us, we were able to give one another the space that we needed while respecting one another's way of coping.

When we came back together, we were then able to pray together, de-brief together, and brainstorm our next steps together. Having Jesus in the center of our lives is what enabled us to stay sane and sensible, happy and hopeful, and fearless and faithful.

Quite honestly, I do not know how anyone can get through life's trials without Jesus on their side. It is tough to hang in there, *real talk*, even with Jesus! Many times I felt as though God had spoken to Satan and said, "Have you considered my servant Twanna?" But the power of the Holy Spirit is amazing. We were able to hang on confidently because of the power of God that flowed through us. Jesus was our rock, our refuge, and our friend.

> What a friend we have in Jesus,
> all our sins and griefs to bear;
> What a privilege to carry
> everything to God in prayer.
> O what peace we often forfeit,
> O what needless pain we bear,
> All because we do not carry

everything to God in prayer.

Have we trials and temptations?
Is there trouble anywhere?
We should never be discouraged;
take it to the Lord in prayer.
Can we find a friend so faithful
who will all our sorrows share?
Jesus knows our every weakness;
take it to the Lord in prayer.

Are we weak and heavy laden,
cumbered with a load of care?
Precious Savior, still our refuge;
take it to the Lord in prayer.
Do thy friends despise, forsake thee?
Take it to the Lord in prayer.
In His arms He'll take and shield thee;
thou wilt find a solace there.

Joseph M. Scriven, 1857

11. IT'S TIME FOR A CHANGE

A change, a change has come over me
He changed my life and now I'm free

He washed away all my sins
and he made me whole
He washed me white as snow
He changed my life complete
and now I sit, I sit at His feet
To do what must be done
I'll work and work until He comes

A wonderful change has come over me
A wonderful change has come over me

Walter Hawkins

I remember listening to the choir belt out those lyrics on Sundays when I was a little girl coming up in St. Paul Baptist Church. I remember the warm feeling, the harmonized voices, and the emotions that ran high whenever that song was sung. I never understood the significance of the song. Listening to the choir sing about change didn't mean much to a little girl who had yet to experience any real change in her life. That was then. Over the years, I learned that true change takes place when you have a deepened, more significant relationship with Jesus Christ. It is the kind of relationship that causes you to trust Him even when you cannot trace Him.

I would like to imagine a life where everything is perfect—being perfect and never having done anything wrong. No heartaches. No struggles. No mistakes. A life where every bill is paid on time and there is always enough money in the bank. A life that has never known disappointment or what it feels like to lose a loved one, to nurture a dying parent, or to console a sick child. Something tells me that while my church choir used to sing the words to this Walter Hawkins song, the congregation was moved because they knew something about life's struggle, about doing things they surely regretted and having God still show up right on time. They knew something about things being one way then having God step in and turn them completely around. Life's challenges have a way of bringing ι knees. *What better posture is there to pray in?*

Nothing brings us closer to God than t... tribulations. The storms, heartaches, and valleys in our lives keep us (most of the time) praying and seeking Him. It's easy to walk with the Lord when you're on the mountain, but it is how you walk with Him in the valley that determines how well you will handle change. This is the critical time of life. This is where true change has an opportunity to take place. We have two decisions to make during this time. We can either let life beat us up and walk in defeat or we can *rest* in the assurance of knowing that despite what challenges may occur in our lives, God has orchestrated it all. He's God. Nothing catches Him by surprise. So if He allows the crucibles of life, surely there is a grace available to us from Him, to overcome it.

We can sometimes think that this attitude is reserved for a certain type of person. That grace is only for those who get it right all the time. That is not at all the case. I have discovered that we all are on this journey of life. God has no respect of persons. I have found Him to be a present help in my time of trouble. Psalm 34:18 states, *"The LORD is near to the brokenhearted and saves those who are crushed in spirit."*

You know what? God has our attention the most when we are going through something that we know we cannot overcome without Him. What is great about God is, He does not hold that against us. In fact, He actually uses it as an opportunity to catapult us to a deeper place with Him.

True change comes about when we determine that our way isn't working and that we have to position ourselves in a different place so that we are prepared to move forward. In order to move forward, we need CHANGE. A change of mind. A change of heart. A change of perspective. And sometimes a change of greater faith. *A wonderful change has come over me.*

12. THE OTHER SIDE OF THE MOUNTAIN

MJ was in the NICU for 193 days. That's over six months in a simulated world. He was in the NICU longer than he was in my womb. One of the hardest parts was dealing with the deaths of the babies in the NICU whose families I had come to know. First was Baby Jada. She was a twin. Like MJ, she and her twin sister, Joy, were very tiny. They seemed to be doing so well. Then one day I learned that she was fighting to stay alive. She did not make it. Her sister was able to hang on.

Next was Baby Emory. He was full term but he was born with a rare disease called posterior urethra dysfunction. His little body was extremely bloated. I had a few casual conversations with his mom during his stay in the NICU. Like me, she was numb from everything that was going on. I remember calling the NICU one night to find out how MJ was doing. I had planned to head to the hospital that evening to visit him as I did on a daily basis. When I called, the nurse told me that MJ was fine but that it was not a good night to come. I knew at that moment that something was wrong. They were not allowed to give out specific information. After months and months of my new normal, by this time I knew the routine. I discovered the next day that Baby Emory had passed away.

I had never attended a funeral for a baby. That is not something that anyone thinks about doing. I had extremely mixed feelings. My own baby was still hanging on with an unsure prognosis. But I felt like it was the least that I could do. It was a graveside service. It was short, moving, and sad. *Lord, I just don't understand.* Baby Emory's mother and I would later cross paths. We are friends today.

Near MJ's latter months in the NICU, he was moved to the front of the unit. Praise God we were getting closer to the exit door. He was now in an open crib and he was moved next to a crib with a little Hispanic baby girl by the name of Rosa. Over her crib hung frilly pink dresses. I thought to myself that it would be several months before she would be able to fit those dresses. I think the dresses gave her mom hope as to what her little girl could look forward to. I came in to visit MJ one day and Rosa was gone. The dresses were gone. Another sad day.

The day finally came for MJ to come home. It was March

18, 2004. I think it was the scariest day of my life! He still seemed very small. By now he had a g-tube in his stomach. His breathing was still supported and he needed medication, steroids, vitamins, and a heart monitor. It was weird because I had grown so accustomed to visiting him in the hospital. That was his home. How would he adjust to a new home? How would we adjust to a third party in the house? What if we made a mistake? *I will trust in the Lord with all my might.*

13. NOT MY WILL

MJ's transition to his new home with his own room was successful. I think he had to learn to embrace the silent nights. No beeping. No whispering. No poking or prodding. He was learning us and we were learning him. We would later discover that MJ had significant delays in the areas of gross motor, fine motor, communication and social-emotional skills. As the months and years went by, they were filled with physical therapists, occupational therapists, and speech therapists to help him along the way. Some good. Some not so good. No major results.

In spite of it all, I have learned that God is a faithful God. Even when we do not understand the hand that life has dealt us, we must learn to play it to the best of our ability. In the game of life, we do not have the luxury of throwing our dealt hand in and requesting another one. It just does not work that way. MJ has been a blessing to my life. His life has taught me many things. It has taught me about real love—the kind that cannot give back to you. It has taught me to trust God when it seems impossible to trace God. It has taught me patience; waiting on the Lord is an art. It has taught me humility; never say what will never happen to you. It has taught me faith; genuine faith operates outside of time.

> This I recall to my mind,
> Therefore I have hope.
> The Lord's lovingkindnesses indeed never cease,
> For His compassions never fail.
> They are new every morning;
> Great is Your faithfulness.
>
> *Lamentations 3:21-23*

Life makes us no promises. God does what He wills. Our response: *dance with the scars.*

AN AFTERWORD

Dear Beloved,

Have you ever heard the phrase, "do as I say, not as I do" Well that is my sentiment to you. In life, we all make mistakes. We do not all make the same mistakes, but we make them nonetheless. It would be so great if we had 20/20 vision into our future. We would be able to catch ourselves before we engaged in unthinkable actions and unimaginable behaviors. We would steer clear of unhealthy relationships and toxic people. If we could delete the errors from the manuscript of our lives, life would be so much better. Unfortunately that is not the case.

To anyone who does not have a personal relationship with the Lord, I want you to know that Jesus longs to be in relationship with you. *If you do not know Jesus as your Lord and savior, i.e., if you do not know without a shadow of doubt that you would go to heaven when you die, then you must first open your mouth and confess Jesus as Lord, believe in your heart that He died and God raised Him from the dead, and invite Him into your heart and life to be your Lord and Savior. "For with the heart a person believes, resulting in righteousness, and with the mouth he confesses, resulting in salvation"* (Romans 10:10).

To young women, I want to say, know who you are in the Lord. Do not let anyone define who you are. Appreciate your individual uniqueness. Do not look for love in the wrong places. Do not replace the love of God with any other kind of love. Do not shun accountability. You are precious in His sight. You are beautiful. You are loved. *"I will give thanks to You, for I am fearfully and wonderfully made; wonderful are Your works, and my soul knows it very well"* (Psalm 139:14).

To young men, I want to say, protect your sisters in the Lord. Value them and handle them with care. Commend them for their walk with the Lord and in the same way, you too strengthen your walk with Him. Ask the Lord to give you a genuine care and concern for them (I Corinthians 12:25).

To those who are going through a difficult or challenging season, I want to say, do not give up! God promises to never leave you nor forsake you. *"We count those blessed who endured. You have heard of the endurance of Job and have seen the outcome of the Lord's dealings, that the Lord is full of compassion and is merciful"* (James 5:11).

And to everyone, God is more than able to carry us from the mishaps, trials, tribulations and even **failures** in our lives, to a place of firm and assuring **faith** in Him. Be encouraged!

Agape,

Twanna

ABOUT THE AUTHOR

Twanna Henderson has a deep passion for seeing the body of Christ grow in the fullness of the Lord. She particularly has a heart for women of all ages, as well as parents of special needs children.

She speaks across the country to audiences for Retreats, Conferences, and Worship Services.

For Booking Ministry Engagements and Book Signings:

Email: RevTwanna@gmail.com or call 704-684-4586

Also, be sure to email or write her and let her know how *Dancing With The Scars* has blessed you.

Ministry Address:
7027 Stillwell Road
Matthews, NC 28105